FORCES
AND MOTION

Peter Lafferty

SCIENCE FACT FILES

FORCES AND MOTION

Peter Lafferty

RAINTREE
STECK-VAUGHN
RSVP ® PUBLISHERS

A Harcourt Company

Austin · New York
www.steck-vaughn.com

Produced by Roger Coote Publishing

Published by Raintree Steck-Vaughn, an imprint of Steck-Vaughn Company

Design and typesetting Victoria Webb
Commissioning Editor Lisa Edwards
Editor Roger Goddard-Coote
Picture Researcher Lynda Lines
Illustrator Alex Pang
Raintree Steck-Vaughn Staff:
Editor Kathy DeVico
Project Manager Max Brinkmann

Library of Congress Cataloging-in-Publication Data
Lafferty, Peter.
    Forces and motion / Peter Lafferty.
    p. cm. — (Science fact files)
    Includes bibliographical references and index.
    Summary: Introduces different types of forces, the laws that govern them, and Einstein's theory of relativity.
    ISBN 0-7398-1007-3
    1. Force and energy—Juvenile literature. 2. Motion—Juvenile literature. [1. Force and energy. 2. Motion.] I. Title. II. Series.
    QC73.4 .L34 2001
    531'.6 21—dc21
                                                                99-044324

Pages 2–3: At a wind farm, the energy of the wind is used to produce electricty.
Title page picture: Skydivers falling toward Earth.

We are grateful to the following for permission to reproduce photographs:
Robert Harding Picture Library 11 (Jeremy Bright); Science Photo Library front cover right (Lawrence Berkeley Laboratory), 9 top (Prof Harold Edgerton), 9 bottom (Philippe Plailly), 13 (Richard Megna/Fundamental Photos), 14 (Michael Dalton/Fundamental Photos), 16 (NASA), 22 (Keith Kent), 24 (Peter Menzel), 27 (Dick Luria), 28 (Adam Hart-Davis), 30 (George Haling), 33 (Steve Grand), 35 (Kaj R. Svensson), 36 top (NASA), 37 (Lawrence Berkeley), 40 (Library of Congress), 41 (Stanford Linear Accelerator Center), 43 (Mehau Kulyk); Stock Market front cover left (David Lawrence), 5, 8, 10–11, 18, 19 (Tom Sanders/Photri), 31 (CH Jones), 36 bottom, 38 (Tom Ives), 39 (David Lawrence); Tony Stone Images 17 (Bob Thomason). Remaining photos are courtesy of Digital Vision.

The statistics given in this book are the most up to date available at the time of going to press.

Printed in Hong Kong

2 3 4 5 6 7 8 9 WKT 05 04 03

CONTENTS

4-19-04 paul 27.14 (19.00)

INTRODUCTION

The world is an ever-changing place, full of activity and movement. The wind blows, moving clouds across the sky. Cars travel along roads. People walk, run, talk, work, and play. None of these things would happen without **forces**.

Anything that causes something to move or changes its motion involves a force. A force is a push or a pull. If you push on an object you are applying a force to the object. If you push hard enough, the object will start to move. If the object is already moving, a force can make it go faster or slower or change the direction in which it moves.

Forces can have other effects, too. A force can stretch an elastic object such as a rubber band. A force can tear paper or change the shape of clay. Pairs of forces can make objects spin.

A yacht on a breezy day is driven along by the force of the wind. A strong wind is needed to push the yacht through the water.

A pole vaulter is lifted over the bar by the elastic force produced by the pole when it is bent.

THE FUNDAMENTAL FORCES
There are really just five kinds of forces. They are called the fundamental, or basic, forces. All other forces are variations of them. The fundamental forces are gravity, electrical force, magnetic force, the strong nuclear force, and the weak nuclear force. Gravitation is the force that attracts all objects to one another. Electrical force is produced by tiny particles that are electrically charged. Magnetic force is the force produced between two moving electric charges. The two nuclear forces are found only inside the center, or **nucleus**, of an **atom**. The strong force holds the nucleus together. The weak force helps break up the nucleus of some atoms in what is called nuclear decay.

This computer display shows the decay, or breakup, of a subatomic particle. Decay such as this is caused by the weak nuclear force.

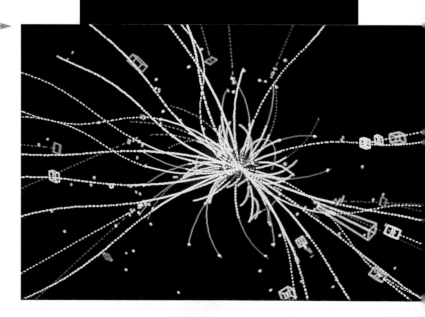

Among the natural forces around us are **gravity** and **friction**. Gravitation is the force that attracts each object in the universe to every other object. It pulls everything on or near Earth—including you—toward Earth's center. Friction is the force that resists the motion of objects that touch. It slows or stops moving things. A rolling ball eventually stops because friction between the ball and the ground brings it to a stop.

GRAVITY

When you drop an object, it falls towards Earth. There is a force pulling the object down that makes it fall when it is released. This force is gravity. It is a force that acts between objects, pulling them together.

The force of gravitation is produced by all objects that have **mass**. Mass is the amount of material in an object—the total of all the atoms and **molecules** it contains. The more mass an object has, the stronger the force of gravitation it produces. The force of gravity produced by Earth is strong because Earth has a large mass.

Mass is not the same as **weight**. The weight of an object is a measure of the force with which Earth's gravity pulls upon it. An object with a large mass has a large weight, because there is a large gravitational force pulling it down towards Earth.

The force of gravity pulls a rock climber down. The force called friction helps him to cling to the cliff face.

FACT FILE

JUMPING ON THE MOON
Because the force of gravity on the Moon is less than on Earth, it is easier to jump on the Moon. A high jumper could jump about six times higher on the Moon than on Earth. On Jupiter, where the gravity is twice as strong as on Earth, a high jumper could jump only about half as high as on Earth.

ISAAC NEWTON (1642–1727)
English scientist Isaac Newton discovered that Earth's gravity reaches to the Moon. He made this important discovery during research conducted from 1665 to 1666. He also explained how the Sun's gravity keeps the planets moving around it, and invented a new type of mathematics, calculus, to describe how objects move.

These boats have been left ashore by the retreating tide. The Moon's gravity causes the tides by pulling the ocean toward it.

Gravity and Distance

Although the mass of an object stays the same wherever it is, its weight can vary. Weight varies because the force of gravity is not the same in all places. The farther objects are from each other, the smaller the force of gravity between them. So if you are flying in an aircraft, you would actually weigh slightly less than you do on the ground because you would be farther from Earth.

The force of gravity on other planets is different from that on Earth. The gravity of planets differs because each planet has a different mass. A massive planet, such as Jupiter, has a strong force of gravity. On Jupiter you would weigh more than twice as much as you do on Earth. On Mercury, which has a smaller mass than Earth, the force of gravity is one-third Earth's. For this reason, on Mercury you would weigh about one-third as much as on Earth.

ELECTRICAL AND MAGNETIC FORCES

These two types of forces are so closely related that they are difficult to separate. Sometimes they are combined and described as a single force, called the electromagnetic force.

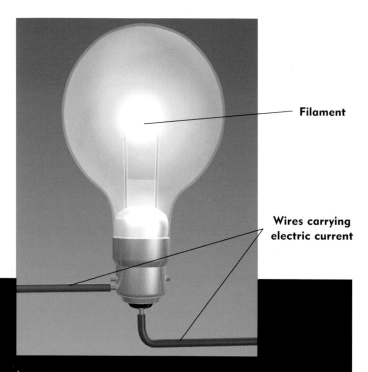

Filament

Wires carrying electric current

Inside a light bulb there is a thin coil of wire called a filament. When electricity flows through it, the filament becomes very hot—about 2,500°C (4,532°F)—and glows brightly.

 **FACT FILE**

ELECTRONS
An electron is a tiny particle that carries a negative electric charge. An electric current is made up of moving electrons. When you switch on an electric light, about 3 trillion electrons pass through the light bulb every second.

Electrical Force

Electrical forces are produced by tiny particles that carry electric **charges**. These electric charges can be either positive or negative. The electrical force between two particles with the same charge pushes the particles away from each other. Particles that have opposite charges are attracted to one another. Like gravity, electrical force can travel through empty space. It is strongest near the object that is producing it.

Some materials become electrically charged when they are rubbed. For example, if you rub a balloon with a woolen cloth, the balloon becomes negatively charged. This happens because tiny particles that are negatively charged, called **electrons**, move from the wool and onto the balloon.

Because the balloon is negatively charged, there is an electrical force attracting it to the positive charges in other objects. The balloon will attract and pick up small pieces of paper, and it may even "stick" to a wall. However, there will also be an electrical force between the balloon and other negatively charged objects. In this case the force will push them apart. If you rub two balloons with a woolen cloth and hang them side by side, you will see that they repel, or push each other away.

Magnetic Force

When two electric charges are moving, they produce a force between them. This is called magnetic force. The charges can be electric currents moving along wires, for example, or they can be electrons moving around the nucleus of an atom. Like electrical force, magnetic force can travel through empty space. It is strongest near the object that is producing it and gets weaker farther away.

Magnets and Poles

Magnets produce magnetic forces. The space around a magnet in which the magnetic force can be felt is called a magnetic field. Some materials can be magnetized—made into magnets. Metals such as iron, nickel, and cobalt magnetize easily. Materials such as paper, glass, and plastic can't be magnetized.

There are two areas on a magnet where the magnetic force is strongest. These areas are called the **magnetic poles**. One pole is called the north pole; if the magnet is hung so that it can rotate, it will turn so that its north pole faces north. The other pole is called the south pole; it faces south if the magnet is allowed to turn.

The two poles of a magnet interact in a predictable way. When the south pole of one magnet is brought near the north pole of another magnet, the poles pull together or attract each other. However, when two north poles, or two south poles, are brought together, they push apart; they repel each other.

Earth is like a giant magnet whose magnetic field extends into space.

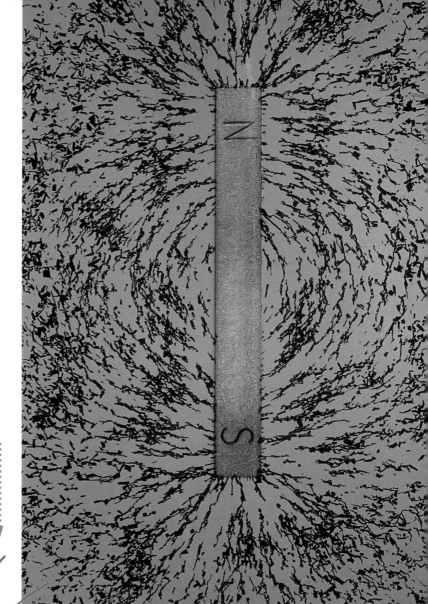

North magnetic pole

Earth

Iron filings, scattered around a magnet, arrange themselves into lines, called "lines of force." They show the direction of the magnetic force around the magnet.

Lines of magnetic force. The magnetic field is strongest where the lines are closest together.

South magnetic pole

13

MEASURING FORCES

orces can be large or small. A small insect produces only a small force to jump a short distance upward. However, the force produced by a space rocket to lift itself into orbit is huge. The rocket needs a much larger force because it has to lift a much greater mass than the insect does.

Forces are often measured in units called **newtons**, named after the scientist Isaac Newton. One newton is defined as the force needed to accelerate a mass of 1 kilogram (2.2 lb) by 1 meter (3.3 ft) per second per second.

Balances

A spring balance, or spring scale, is used to measure weight and other forces. A weight hung on the hook of the spring balance, applies a force to the hook. As

A spring balance

A triple-beam balance is used to weigh chemicals, such as the powder in the pan.

As the wooden block is pulled along, the scale on the spring balance shows how much the force is used to overcome friction.

Block of wood

Spring balance

Smooth surface

the spring inside is stretched by the weight or force, the marker moves along the scale. The scale is marked in newtons, kilograms, or pounds.

Scientists often use a different kind of balance. It has a beam, resting on a pivot at its center, with a small pan hung on each end. The substance to be weighed is placed in one pan. Weights of different sizes are placed in the other. The beam is horizontal when the objects in the pans have equal masses.

TEST FILE

MEASURING FRICTION

You can use a spring balance to measure the force of friction. Attach the spring balance to a block of wood placed on a smooth surface. Slowly pull the spring balance until the block begins to move. What amount of force is needed to start the block moving? How much force is needed to keep the block moving? Try the experiment again on a rough surface (tape some sandpaper to the smooth surface). How much force is needed this time?

More force is needed to overcome friction when the block is pulled across a rough surface.

Sandpaper

COMBINED AND BALANCED FORCES

The U.S. Air Force Blackbird in flight. The Blackbird holds the world speed record for a jet-powered aircraft—over 3,500 kilometers (2,175 mi) per hour.

FACT FILE

VECTORS AND SCALARS

A quantity that has both size and direction is called a vector. Force, **velocity**, and **acceleration** are all vector quantities.

A quantity that has only size is called a scalar. Mass, **speed**, time, energy, and **density** are scalar quantities.

Most objects have more than one force acting on them. For instance, an aircraft in flight has several forces acting on it at any one time. Its weight is pulling it toward Earth, the flow of air above and under its wings is lifting it upward, and the force from its engines is pushing it forward. The pilot has to balance these forces to make the aircraft fly in the right direction. However, it is often hard to judge the overall effect of several forces acting at the same time.

Resultant Force

Sometimes, when only two forces act on an object, it is easy to see the overall effect. If a force of 3 newtons and another force of 4 newtons both pull an object in the same direction, the overall effect is the same as a single force of 7 newtons pulling in the same direction. The overall force that has the same effect as several forces acting on an object is called the **resultant force**. In this case, the resultant force is 7 newtons, acting in the same direction as the combining forces. The direction of the forces is important. Force has a direction as well as a size and is known as a vector quantity.

It is also easy to see the overall effect when two equal forces act in opposite directions. Equal forces acting in opposite directions cancel each other out. This happens, for example, when opposing tug-of-war teams pull with the same force; the resultant force is zero and neither team moves.

The combined force of three tugs pulls a floating oil platform. The largest tugs can pull with a force of 25,000 newtons.

Force A (3 newtons)

Resultant force (6 newtons)

Force B (4 newtons)

A parallelogram of forces. The two shorter arrows represent the size and direction of forces A and B. The longer arrow shows the size and direction of the resultant force.

The Parallelogram of Forces

When two forces pull at an angle to each other, the overall effect is harder to predict. In these cases we have to draw a diagram, called a parallelogram of forces, to find the resultant force. The sides of the parallelogram are drawn to represent the size and direction of the forces—the larger the force, the longer the side of the parallelogram. The diagonal of the parallelogram represents the size and direction of the resultant force.

A weight lifter must push up with a force that balances the downward force of gravity.

 **TEST FILE**

FINDING THE CENTER OF GRAVITY

To find the center of gravity of a flat object such as a piece of cardboard, hang the cardboard from a hook. Then hang a thread with a weight on the end from a hook. Let them swing freely. When they have stopped swinging, draw a line on the cardboard along the thread. Now hang the cardboard and the thread from the same hook, but hang the cardboard from a different point. Draw another line along the thread. The center of gravity is where the two lines cross.

Balanced Forces

When opposing tug-of-war teams pull with equal force, nothing happens. The forces cancel each other, and the resultant force is zero. When the resultant of two or more forces is zero, the forces are balanced. They are said to be in **equilibrium**.

Balanced forces are very common. For example, when you sit on a chair, your weight is pushing down on the chair, but the chair pushes upward with an equal force. The two forces are balanced and are in equilibrium.

The forces in a building or bridge must be balanced; if they were not, the building would collapse. A bridge, for example, must support its own weight and the weight of the traffic crossing it. These downward forces must be balanced by upward forces, which are often provided by supports at the end of the bridge.

A moving object can be in equilibrium, too, if the forces acting on it are balanced. A car that is moving at a constant **velocity** (speed in a certain direction) is in equilibrium because the force of its engine and the force of friction are balanced.

Center of Gravity

If you balance a pencil on your finger, the forces acting on the pencil are balanced. Your finger provides an upward force to balance the weight of the pencil. But you can only balance the pencil if your finger supports it at the center point. It is as if the weight of the pencil is concentrated in the center of the pencil, at a point called the **center of gravity**. An object can be balanced only if its support is directly below its center of gravity.

FACT FILE

TERMINAL VELOCITY

When an object is falling through the air, it accelerates (its speed increases) as it falls. This is because its weight is pulling it downward. There is also a force pushing upward on the object, caused by air resistance, or drag. The faster the object falls, the greater the drag. Eventually, the drag pushing upward becomes equal to the weight pulling downward. The forces on the object are now balanced, so it stops accelerating. It continues falling at a steady speed, known as its terminal speed or terminal velocity.

Skydivers normally fall at a terminal velocity of about 200 km (124 mi) per hour when their arms and legs are spread out. But if a skydiver turns to fall head-down, there is less drag and the terminal velocity increases to about 300 km (186 mi) per hour.

Skydivers falling at terminal velocity

SPEED, VELOCITY, AND ACCELERATION

The **speed** of a moving object is the distance it travels in a certain amount of time. Speed is usually measured in kilometers or miles per hour. The cheetah is the fastest of all land animals. It can run at speeds up to 100 kilometers (62 mi) per hour, which means that it would take one hour to travel 100 kilometers (62 mi) if it kept going at the same speed. This speed is called the average speed.

The speed shown on a car's speedometer is the speed at a particular moment, which is called its instantaneous speed. The car will go faster at some times than at others. It will speed up, or accelerate, at some times. At other times, the car will slow down, or decelerate.

This car is traveling at a constant speed.

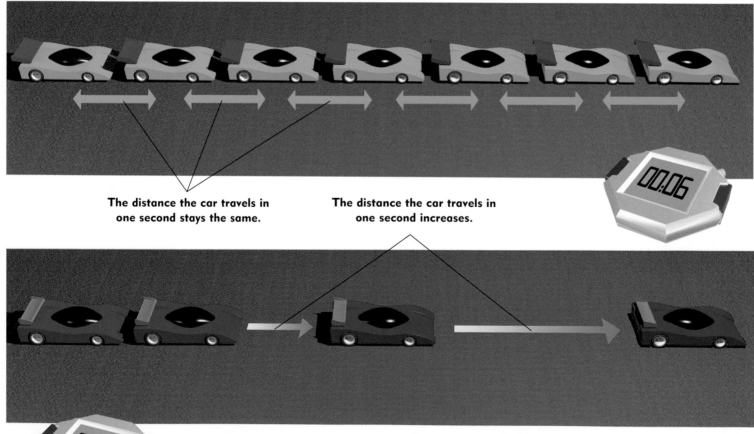

The distance the car travels in one second stays the same.

The distance the car travels in one second increases.

This car is accelerating.

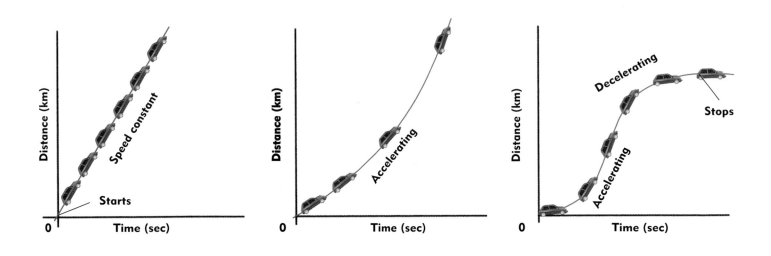

FACT FILE

SPEED GRAPHS
It is possible to show speed in the form of a graph. The three graphs above show the distance traveled by a car plotted against the time taken. The graph on the left shows a car traveling at constant speed. The middle graph shows a car that is accelerating. The right-hand graph shows a car that starts moving, accelerates, decelerates, and then stops.

Velocity and Acceleration

Velocity is often thought to mean the same as speed. In fact, the two are slightly different. Velocity (like force) is a vector quantity, which means it has both size and direction (see Fact File, page 16). Velocity is speed in a certain direction: The velocity of an object changes when the direction in which it is moving changes—even if its speed stays the same. (In everyday life, we normally talk about the speed of an object rather than its velocity, unless the direction in which it is moving is important.)

Acceleration is the change (increase or decrease) in an object's velocity in a certain time. Falling objects accelerate, or speed up, as they fall. On Earth, the acceleration of a falling object (caused by gravity) is 9.8 meters (32 ft) per second per second. This means that a falling object gains an extra 9.8 meters (32 ft) per second of downward speed every second. If there were no air resistance, all falling objects would fall at exactly the same rate. Astronaut Alan Shepard proved this in 1971 when he visited the Moon, which has no atmosphere. He dropped a hammer and a feather at the same time. They fell side by side and hit the ground together.

With no air resistance, these balls would fall at exactly the same rate. In practice, air resistance makes the pink ball fall slightly more slowly (shown by the curved path) than the blue one.

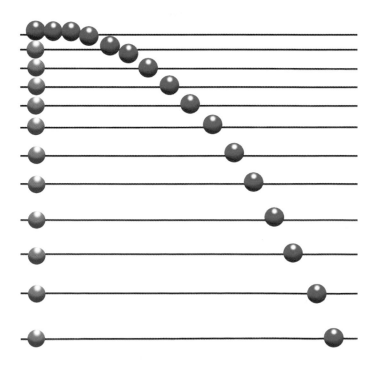

THE LAWS OF MOTION

When the position of an object changes, we say that motion has occurred. Motion can also mean that an object stays in the same position but changes its orientation (turns to face in a different direction). A force is needed to start a stationary object moving, but no force is needed to keep a moving object in motion—as long as there are no other forces acting on it.

The Thrust SuperSonic Car, the first car to travel faster than sound, accelerates according to Newton's second law.

FACT FILE

NEWTON'S LAWS OF MOTION
In the late 1770s, Isaac Newton put forward three laws of motion that explained exactly how forces change an object's motion.

Newton's first law says that an object will remain at rest or continue to move at a constant speed in a constant direction unless it is acted upon by an outside force.

Newton's second law states that if a force acts on an object, the object will accelerate in the direction of the force. The greater the force, the greater the acceleration it produces. The greater the mass of the object, the less the acceleration produced by the force.

Newton's third law states that forces act in pairs: for every action, there is an equal and opposite reaction. When you push or pull an object, your force (called the action force) meets an equal and opposite force (called the reaction force) produced by the object.

Ball thrown forward

Skateboard rolls backward

If you stood on a skateboard and threw a ball forward in front of you, the skateboard would move backward, illustrating Newton's third law of motion.

This fact is shown by spacecraft, which can travel vast distances through space. If no force acts on a craft, its speed and direction of motion will remain unchanged. The craft doesn't experience any air resistance, or drag, to slow it down, because there is no atmosphere in space.

Inertia and Momentum

All objects have a tendency to resist being moved or to resist changes in their speed or direction of motion. This tendency is called **inertia**. The greater the mass of an object, the greater its inertia. This is why a heavy object needs a greater force to start or stop it moving than a lighter object. The heavy object has more mass—and so more inertia—than the light object.

Moving objects have **momentum**. Momentum is equal to the force that would be necessary to stop the object from moving. Momentum depends on the object's mass and velocity.

TEST FILE

ACTION AND REACTION

Put vinegar inside a plastic drink bottle; there should be just enough vinegar so that none runs out when the bottle is laid on its side. Now wrap a teaspoonful of baking powder in tissue paper, and twist the ends tightly. Push the powder into the bottle. Quickly put a cork in the bottle top and place the bottle on two round pencils and wait. The vinegar and the powder will react together, making carbon dioxide gas. When enough gas has been produced, it will blow the cork out of the bottle with a bang. The bottle will run backward along the pencils while the cork flies forward.

WARNING: Have an adult help you with this experiment. Make sure that the cork does not hit anyone when it flies out of the bottle. (Point the cork toward a blank wall or place the bottle in a bathtub.)

The rider is thrown over the neck of a horse as it stops suddenly, illustrating Newton's first law.

FORCES, WORK, AND ENERGY

Forces and **work** go together. Work is done when a force moves something. The amount of work done is related to the size of the force and the distance the object is moved in the direction of the force. The greater the force and the greater the distance, the more work is done.

Work is measured in units called joules. One joule is the work done when a force of 1 newton moves an object through a distance of 1 meter. The joule was named after the English scientist James Joule, who first realized, around 1840, that work produces heat, and that heat is a form of **energy**.

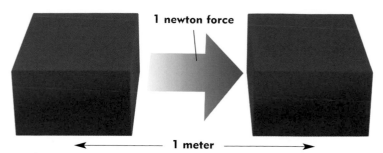

One joule of energy is used when a force of 1 newton moves through a distance of 1 meter.

Solar-powered cars. Solar energy, the energy of sunlight, is changed into other forms of energy in a series of energy transformations. Mechanical energy eventually moves the car.

Energy

Energy is the ability to do work. Work cannot be done without energy. Like work, energy is measured in joules. There are two basic types of energy—kinetic and potential. Kinetic energy is the energy that a moving object has because of its motion. The

Water flows onto wheel

Energy of moving water turns wheel

Water at the top of the water wheel has potential energy (because it is above the ground). Water entering the wheel has kinetic energy (because it is moving). Some of this kinetic energy is used to turn the water wheel.

amount of kinetic energy an object has is related to its mass and its velocity. The greater the mass and the greater the velocity of the object, the greater its kinetic energy.

Potential energy is the stored energy an object has because of its position. Potential energy is equal to the amount of work that was done to put the object in that position. An object that is placed high above the ground—at the top of a tall building, for example—has potential energy because work was needed to put it there, and it will do work if it falls down.

Energy comes in various forms, including gravitational, thermal, chemical, and electrical energy, but they are all basically different forms of kinetic and potential energy. For example, the thermal energy, or heat, of an object is really the kinetic energy of all its atoms; the faster the atoms move, the more heat the object has.

Transformation of Energy

Energy can transform, or change from one form to another. For example, if an object is dropped, its potential energy changes into kinetic energy as it falls. Chemical energy—a type of potential energy—can be changed into kinetic energy in a car engine: The chemical energy of the fuel is transformed into mechanical energy when the car moves.

FACT FILE

HOW MUCH ENERGY?
Kinetic energy contained in a car moving at 110 kilometers (68 mi) per hour: 5,000,000 joules.
Heat energy of a kettleful of boiling water: 700,000 joules.
Electrical energy in a charged battery: 2,000,000 joules.
Chemical energy in food eaten in one day: 11,000,000 joules.
Chemical energy in 1 gallon (4.5 liters) of gasoline: 35,000,000 joules.

A nuclear power plant changes the nuclear energy of atoms into electrical energy.

Conserving Energy

When you throw a ball upward, the moving ball has kinetic energy. However, the ball slows down as it goes higher; its kinetic energy is gradually decreasing. At its highest point, the ball is motionless for a brief moment. At that point, the ball has no kinetic energy. This does not mean that its energy has disappeared. Energy cannot disappear; it can only change its form.

At the ball's highest point, its kinetic energy is converted into potential energy. As the ball falls back down to you, its potential energy is changed back

A perpetual motion machine designed in 1834. It was thought that once the wheel was started spinning, the movement of the weights would keep it turning forever. Of course, that is not the case, because some energy is lost as a result of friction, causing the wheel to slow down and eventually stop.

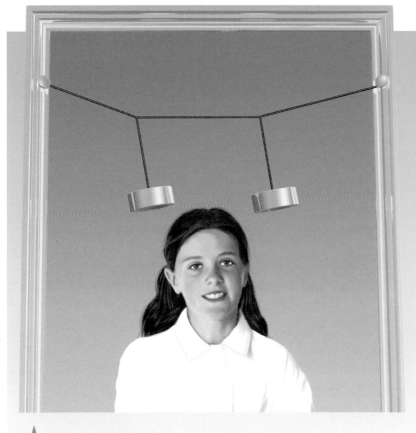

The still pendulum starts to swing because it gains energy from the moving pendulum.

TEST FILE

SYMPATHETIC PENDULUMS

Stretch a string between two supports. Now hang two pendulums, each made from a weight and a length of string, from the string between the supports. Make sure the two pendulums are the same length. Start one of the pendulums swinging.

The second pendulum will soon start to swing, too. When this happens, the first pendulum will almost stop. Then the situation will reverse: the second pendulum will almost stop and the other pendulum will start swinging again. Energy is transferred between the pendulums, although the total amount of energy (minus that converted into heat energy) remains the same.

into kinetic energy. If we don't count the energy that is lost through air resistance, the ball returns to you with the same amount kinetic energy as it had when you threw it.

In practice the ball would return to the ground with slightly less energy than it had when it was thrown. Some of the ball's energy is converted into heat energy as the ball collides with air particles. The ball slows slightly and the air is warmed slightly. If this heat energy is taken into account, the total amount of energy does not change at all during the ball's flight.

This example illustrates an important law of science, called the law of conservation of energy. This law states that energy cannot be created or destroyed, only changed from one form to another. In other words the total amount of energy in the universe is always the same.

When two billard balls collide, their total energy and momentum are the same after the collision as before.

MACHINES

Using a system of pulleys, it is possible for one person to lift a very heavy weight.

Levers

Some machines can change a small movement into a large one. An oar on a rowboat does this. The rower moves the inner end of the oar a small distance, and the other end of the oar moves a much larger distance. This type of simple machine is called a lever. Levers can magnify a force if the turning point, or **fulcrum**, is positioned between the load and the effort forces. Such levers are found in scissors, nut crackers, and crowbars.

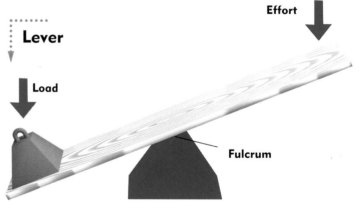

Lever

Effort

Load

Fulcrum

A machine is a device that is designed to make work easier to do. A pulley is a simple machine. It consists of a length of rope wound around a wheel that is fixed to a support, such as a beam. A load or weight is attached to one end of the rope, and the other end of the rope is pulled. It is easier to pull down on the rope than to lift the weight directly upward. Pulleys with more than one wheel allow a small force, called the effort, to lift a heavy load. These types of pulleys are force magnifiers.

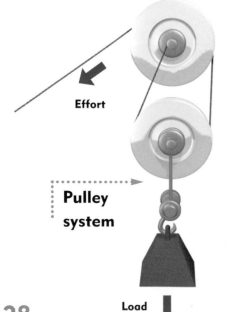

Effort

Pulley system

Load

Inclined Planes and Wheels and Axles

Other simple machines are the inclined plane (or slope) and the wheel and axle. A road winding around a mountain is an example of an inclined plane. It is easier to walk up the winding road than to climb directly to the mountain top. Of course, you

FACT FILE

POWER
The **power** of a machine is the rate at which it can do work. Power is measured in units called watts, named after the Scottish engineer James Watt, who made the first practical steam engine in 1769. One watt is equal to 1 joule per second.

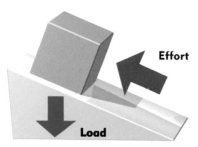

Inclined plane

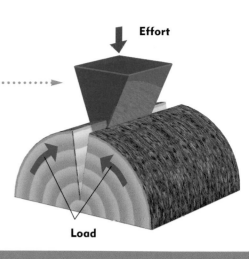

Wedge
A wedge is a machine. It can be used to push things apart or split them.

must travel a greater distance when using the road, but the effort needed is less.

A wheel and axle is a large disk, or wheel,

attached to a thin shaft, or axle. This machine magnifies a force because the wheel is larger than the axle. When you turn the wheel, the axle moves with greater force than that applied to the wheel. A door knob is an example of a wheel and axle.

Wheel and axle

Gears are simple machines based on the wheel and axle.

ARCHIMEDES
Archimedes was an ancient Greek scientist. He lived around 287–212 B.C. in the town of Syracuse, Sicily. He studied how levers and pulleys worked. He was also a skilled mathematician, finding ways to calculate the area of a circle and proving many theorems in geometry.

Archimedes is credited with inventing a machine to lift water from rivers. It consisted of a screw wrapped around an axle in a cylinder. Turning the screw lifted water up inside the cylinder.

TURNING FORCE

If a nut has been screwed onto a bolt tightly, it is difficult to undo with your fingers because you can't apply enough force to the nut to make it turn. However, a wrench can make the job easier. A wrench grips the nut tightly, and its long handle produces a large turning effect. The turning effect of a force around a particular point is called the **moment** of the force. The greater the force, and the farther it is from the turning point, the greater is its turning effect, or moment.

A long wrench can create a large turning force. The longer the wrench, the tighter the nut it can undo.

Stable equilibrium. This object with a weight in the bottom is stable. When tilted slightly, its weight pulls it back to its original position.

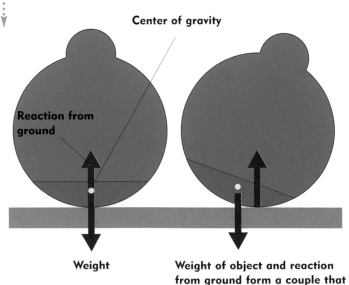

Center of gravity

Reaction from ground

Weight

Weight of object and reaction from ground form a couple that turns the object upright.

Couples

When you turn a car steering wheel, you use two forces. You push on one side of the wheel, and pull on the other side with equal force. A pair of equal but opposite forces acting in parallel lines is called a couple. The greater the forces, and the greater the distance between them, the greater is the turning effect.

Equilibrium

If you sit on a seesaw, your weight produces a turning effect, or moment, around the fulcrum on which the seesaw rests. If someone else sits on the other end, his or her weight produces a moment in the opposite direction. If the opposing moments are equal, they cancel each other out. The seesaw is balanced, or in equilibrium.

An object is said to be in stable equilibrium if, when it is tilted slightly, it returns to its original position. An object that falls over when it is tilted slightly is in unstable equilibrium. An object is in neutral equilibrium if, when moved slightly, it stays in its new position. A ball on a flat table is an example of something that is in neutral equilibrium.

A large valve at a chemical plant is turned by applying two equal but opposite forces, called a couple.

Unstable equilibrium. When tilted slightly, the object's weight pulls it away from its original position.

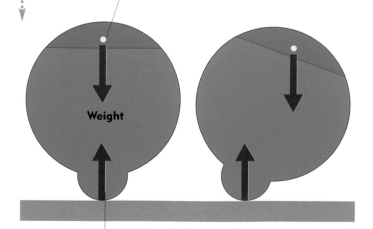

Center of gravity

Weight

Reaction from ground

Weight of object and reaction from ground form a couple that turns the object farther over

Neutral equilibrium: A ball on a flat table is unaffected by a slight change of position.

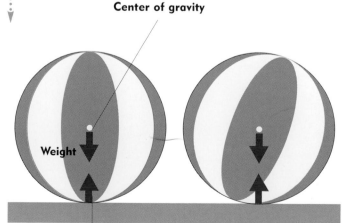

Center of gravity

Weight

Reaction from ground

Weight of object and reaction from ground are in line, so there is no couple. Objects stays in new position.

PERIODIC MOTION

When a pendulum is pushed gently, it will swing from side to side. The side-to-side movements will continue for a long time. These movements are regular—they always take the same length of time, except when the swings are very large. Regular back and forth movements like these are called **vibrations or oscillations**. Any motion like this, which repeats itself at regular intervals, is called a periodic motion.

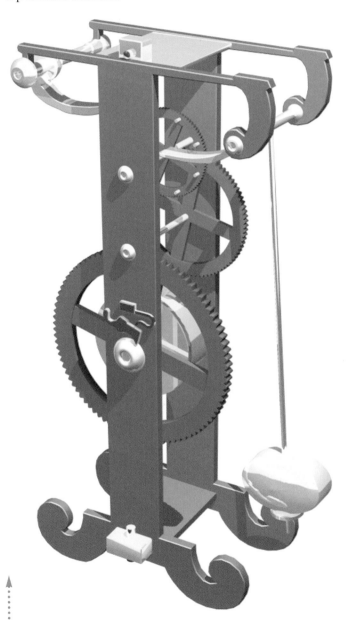

An early metronome. Its regular ticking helped musicians play at a steady pace.

Frequency

Each complete movement of a pendulum—from one side to the other and back again—is called a cycle. The time taken for one cycle is known as a **period**.

The number of cycles of a motion in one second is called the **frequency**. Frequency is measured in units called hertz, after the German scientist Heinrich Hertz, who discovered radio waves in 1888. One hertz equals one cycle per second.

This clockworks, designed by Galileo Galilei in the seventeenth century, uses a swinging weight, or pendulum, to regulate the movement of the hands.

FACT FILE

ANIMAL SOUNDS
A howler monkey can produce sounds with a frequency of 400–6,000 hertz. Bats emit sounds with frequencies up to 90,000 hertz.

Humans can hear sounds with frequencies in the range 2–20,000 hertz. Cats can hear sounds up to 25,000 hertz, and dogs up to 35,000 hertz.

Resonance

Vibrations normally die down after a time, usually because of friction or air resistance. But sometimes vibrations can build up, becoming larger and larger. This effect is called resonance, and it occurs when a vibrating object is given extra energy in a regular way. If you sit on a playground swing and someone gives you a push, you will swing back and forth. The size (or **amplitude**) of each swing will get shorter and shorter until you stop. But if you are given a push at the end of each swing, the amplitude will increase.

Resonance can occur when soldiers march across a bridge. The soldiers' feet make the bridge vibrate. If the soldiers' steps have the correct rhythm, the vibrations will become larger and larger.

Waves

Vibrations travel in waves. When a small wave or ripple moves across a pond, floating leaves vibrate up and down. This action shows that the waves carry energy from one place to another. Sound and light are types of energy that travel in waves. Sound waves are vibrations of the molecules in the air. Light waves are vibrations of the electric and magnetic forces that spread out from electrically charged objects and magnets.

A nuclear magnetic resonance scanner uses magnetic forces and vibrations of particles inside the body to form images of tissues inside the body.

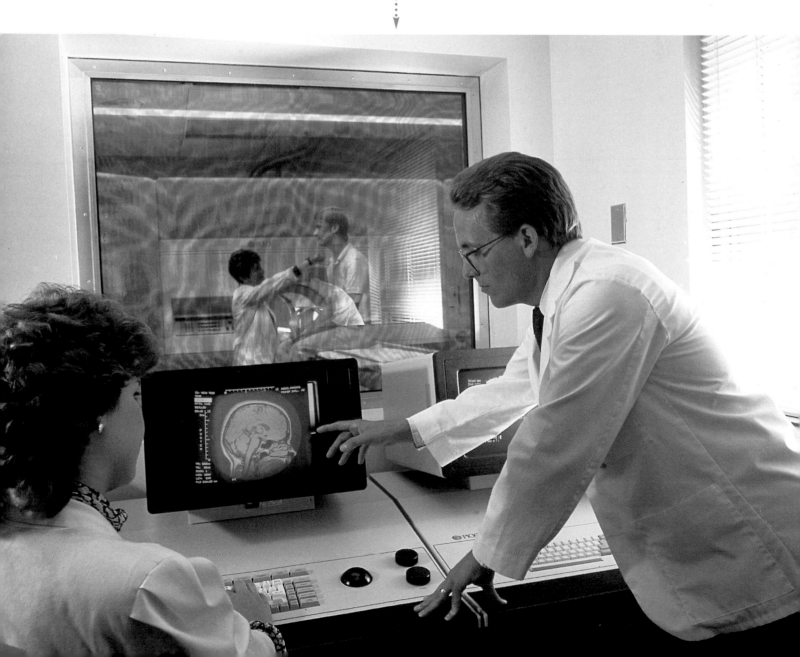

Circular Motion

An object moving round and round in a circle at the same speed is an example of a type of periodic motion known as uniform circular motion. It is an unusual type of motion because the object is always accelerating but it never changes its speed.

On pages 20–21 we saw that speed is the distance an object travels in a certain time and that velocity is speed in a particular direction. Acceleration is the change in an object's velocity in a certain time. From these definitions we can see that an object can accelerate simply by changing its direction, because changing direction means changing velocity. When an object moves in a circle at a fixed speed, it is constantly changing direction and therefore constantly changing velocity, or accelerating.

An astronaut floating in space may appear to be motionless. However, he is really moving in a circle or orbit around the Earth.

Centripetal Force

We know that an object can move or change its motion only if it is acted on by a force. So when an object moves in a circle, there must be a force acting on it. If you whirl a ball around your head on a string, you can feel the force. You have to pull inward on the string to keep the ball moving in a circle. The force that keeps an object moving in a circle is called centripetal force. It continually pulls the object inward so that it follows a circular path.

If the string were to break while you were twirling the ball around your head, the centripetal force would no longer exist. The ball would then move according to Newton's first law of motion: It would move off in a straight line at a steady speed. The ball would continue to move with the speed and in the direction that it was traveling when the string broke. A similar action occurs when a discus thrower spins round and round and then releases the discus.

Making an object move in a circle does not produce a force that acts outward, away from the center of the circle. When people take a loop-the-loop ride at an amusement park, they feel as if there is a force (often called the centrifugal force) pressing them into their seat. What they are actually feeling is the seat pressing in on them: This is the centripetal force, acting toward the center, which makes them move in a circle.

When on a loop-the-loop ride, you can feel the centripetal force that makes you move in a circle. It presses the seat against you.

Angular Momentum

The blades of a fan continue to spin for a while even after the power supply has been turned off. The movement occurs because the blades have momentum. This type of momentum is called angular momentum because the blades are moving in a circle rather than in a straight line. However, angular momentum is like linear (or "straight line") momentum. The more angular momentum an object has, the harder it is to stop the object's movement.

The angular momentum of an object depends upon its mass and how fast it is spinning. The more mass it has, and the faster it is spinning, the harder it is to stop the spinning. But the angular momentum of an object also depends upon the object's shape and size. If two wheels have the same mass but different diameters, the larger wheel will have more angular momentum if both are rotating at the same speed.

In a hurricane, winds spiral around a central region called the eye. The speed of the winds increases as they approach the eye.

A spinning ice skater starts with her arms held wide. When she draws in her arms, she spins faster.

TEST FILE

MAKE A WHIRLPOOL

Fill a clear plastic bottle with water and put in some small pieces of colored paper. Hold the bottle upside down over a basin and quickly remove the top. Watch the movements of the paper. The paper and water should flow in a circular pattern before pouring out of the bottle. Does the paper speed up as it runs through the hole? Can you make the water move in a clockwise, as well as a counterclockwise, direction?

Like linear momentum, the angular momentum of an object is conserved—it stays the same unless a force acts on the object. This situation produces some amazing effects. In storms such as tornadoes and hurricanes, winds blow around a central region or "eye." The winds blow in spirals, getting closer and closer to the center. The nearer they get to the center, the more they speed up in order to conserve their angular momentum. These winds can reach speeds of 450 kilometers (280 mi) per hour.

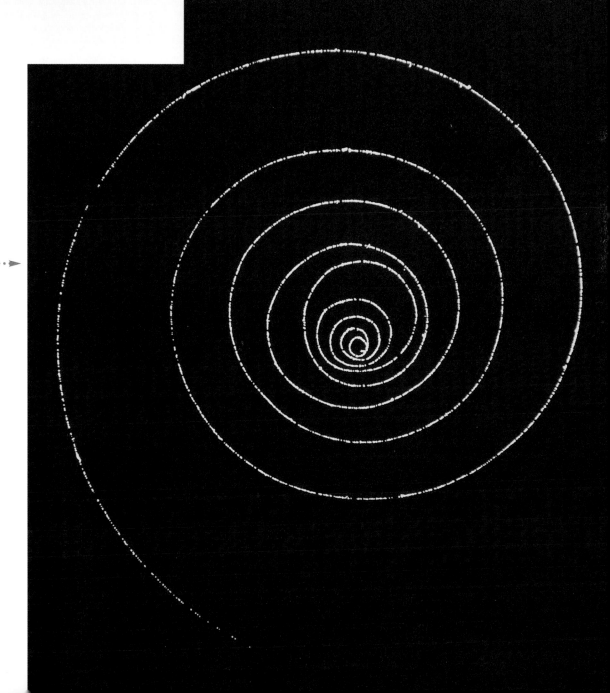

An electron moves in a spiral path near a strong magnet. As the electron slows down, the spiral curls more tightly together.

FORCES IN FLUIDS

When a force is applied to the surface of an object, **pressure** occurs. Pressure is the force acting on a certain area. The greater the force acting on an area, the higher the pressure. The larger the area a force acts over, the lower the pressure. Pressure is measured in pounds per square inch, kilograms per square centimeter, or pascals. One pascal is a pressure that exists when one newton of force acts over an area of one square meter. The pascal is named after French scientist and mathematician Blaise Pascal.

FACT FILE

AIR PRESSURE

At sea level, the average pressure of the atmosphere is about 100,000 pascals (14.7 pounds per square inch). This pressure is produced by the weight of the air. At a height of 6 kilometers (3.7 mi), atmospheric pressure is only about half as great. At 16 kilometers (10 mi), it is one-tenth of the pressure at sea level, and at 100 kilometers (62 mi) it is one-millionth of the pressure.

The difference occurs partly because the higher you go in the atmosphere the less air there is above you, which means there is less weight and, therefore, less pressure. It is also because the air becomes less dense the higher up you go. (See the Fact File on Density on the opposite page.)

Pressure in the water supply drives the spray higher.

Upthrust

If an object is in a fluid, the pressure of the fluid exerts an upward force, called the upthrust, on the object. An object floats when the upthrust equals the weight of the object. An object sinks when its weight is greater than the upthrust and rises when the upthrust is greater than the weight.

The ancient Greek scientist Archimedes discovered that the upthrust on an object always equals the weight of the fluid that has been displaced (pushed aside) by the object. This rule is called Archimedes' Principle. It explains why a ship made of steel can float on water. The ship floats because it is big enough to displace a large quantity of water, creating an upthrust that is equal to its weight.

Pressure and Depth

Any fluid (a liquid or a gas) exerts a pressure on objects within it. The pressure in any fluid depends on the depth of the fluid. The greater the depth, the greater the pressure. At a depth of 120 meters (394 ft), the pressure under the ocean is enough to crush a diver. At 10,000 meters (6.2 mi) under the ocean, the pressure is equivalent to the weight of an elephant on an area the size of a postage stamp.

Lift

Wing

Air flows more slowly under the bottom surface of wing.

As air flows around an airplane wing, an upward force called lift is produced.

Air flows faster over the top surface of wing because it must travel farther than air passing under the wing.

Moving Fluids

When a fluid is moving, the pressure within it decreases as the speed of flow increases. This explains why an aircraft wing produces a lifting force. As the aircraft moves through the air, air flows faster over the curved top surface of the wing than over the flat bottom surface. Therefore, there is less pressure above the wing than below it, and the wing is pushed upward.

A hydrofoil boat has structures (hydrofoils) beneath its hull that act in the same way as an airplane wing. Water flows faster over the top surface of the hydrofoil than over the bottom. The hydrofoil is pushed upward, lifting the boat above the water.

In order to take off, an aircraft has to build up speed on the runway until its wings produce enough lift.

FACT FILE

DENSITY

The density of an object depends on the mass of the atoms and **molecules** it is made of, and on the object's volume —how much space it takes up. One cubic meter of water is denser than one cubic meter of air because water has more mass than an equal volume of air. On the other hand, one kilogram of air has a much greater volume than one kilogram of water.

EINSTEIN AND RELATIVITY

Around the beginning of the twentieth century, the German scientist Albert Einstein wondered what it would be like to travel as fast as light. What would happen, for example, if a person looking in a mirror were to suddenly move off at such high speed? Would the person be able to see his or her refection in the mirror? One might think that if the person moved faster than light, the light reflected from the mirror would not be able to catch up with the person. So, he or she would not see the reflection.

Einstein concluded that this is ridiculous. He decided that it must be impossible for anything to travel as fast as light. The speed of light must be Nature's ultimate speed limit. This simple idea led Einstein to many astonishing conclusions.

Special Relativity

Einstein came to realize that at very high speeds—near the speed of light—things don't always behave in ways we expect. Common-sense ideas are of no use. At near-light speeds, distances and objects shrink, time slows down, and clocks run slow. The mass of an object increases at high speeds, which means that as its speed increases an object needs a larger and larger force to make it accelerate. Einstein's ideas, called the special theory of relativity, also showed that matter could be converted into energy. This discovery led to the development of nuclear power and nuclear weapons.

Albert Einstein, who explained that nothing can travel faster than light

HISTORY FILE

ALBERT EINSTEIN (1879–1955)
Einstein was born in Ulm, a town in southern Germany. At school, he was considered rather slow by his teachers, but he was fascinated by science. He is now regarded as one of the greatest scientists of all time. His special theory of relativity, which dealt with high-speed motion, was published in 1905. He was awarded the Nobel Prize in physics in 1921. In 1933 Einstein moved to the United States.

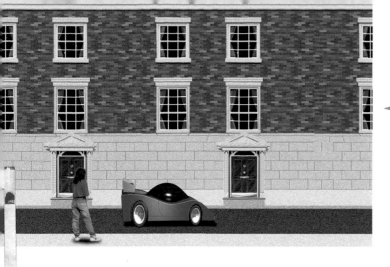

If a car could move nearly as fast as light, it would appear contracted or squashed to a stationary onlooker.

But to the driver, the houses along the roadside would seem contracted.

In everyday life, we never travel fast enough to notice the strange effects Einstein described, but his ideas have been proved correct in many experiments. For example, very accurate clocks called atomic clocks have been flown around the world in high-speed aircraft. When they were compared with atomic clocks that had not been moved, the clocks that had been in the aircraft were found to have slowed down due to their fast motion.

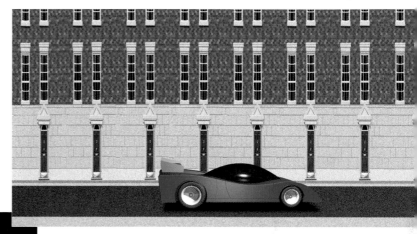

 **FACT FILE**

FAST-MOVING MASS

According to Einstein's theory of relativity, the mass of an object increases when it moves. The mass of an object is increased by 15 percent if it travels at half the speed of light, and by 100 percent if the object travels at nine-tenths of the speed of light.

A particle accelerator speeds up subatomic particles and reveals the effects predicted by Albert Einstein.

SPACE-TIME, GRAVITY, AND BLACK HOLES

Albert Einstein discovered that, in some ways, space is rather like a rubber sheet. If a heavy object is placed on a rubber sheet, the sheet forms a hollow or dip around the object. Then, if a light object, such as a marble, is placed on the sheet, it will roll toward the heavy object. The objects act as if gravity is pulling them together. Using this simple idea, Einstein was able to explain how gravity is caused and to make some amazing predictions.

Of course, Einstein didn't think that there really is a rubber sheet stretching through space. But he showed that there is something called "space-time" that acts in a similar way. Space-time is a combination of space and time. It is difficult to visualize, and Einstein had to use complicated mathematics to describe it.

Using his idea, now called the general theory of relativity, Einstein showed that light is affected by gravity. He predicted that beams of light from distant stars would be bent by the gravity of the galaxies that they pass between. In 1919 this prediction was proved correct.

FACT FILE

A TIGHT SQUEEZE
To form a black hole, our Sun would have to collapse until it shrank to a diameter of 6 kilometers (3.7 mi) (compared to 1,392,000 kilometers [865,000 mi] now). The Earth would have to be squeezed into a diameter of 18 millimeters (.06 in) (down from 12,756 kilometers [7,926 mi]) to form a black hole.

Photo taken by the Hubble Space Telescope

Light beams from star bent by gravity

Galaxy

Distant star

Images of star

Hubble Space Telescope

Gravity affects light beams according to Einstein. Light beams from distant stars are bent by the gravity of closer large galaxies. This produces multiple images of a distant star.

An artist's impression of glowing gas
spiraling into a black hole

The galaxy M51, which is thought to
have a black hole at its center

FUTURE FILE

WORMHOLES

According to Einstein's theory, there may
be tunnels through space-time, called
wormholes. In the future we might be
able to use them to travel to distant
parts of the universe. However, some
scientists think wormholes would
collapse before they could be used
in this way.

Black Holes

Perhaps the most amazing prediction of Einstein's
theory was black holes. These are extremely dense
objects in space with immensely strong gravity. A
black hole forms when a large star shrinks down to a
small point under the force of its own gravity. It is as
if a very small, extremely heavy ball were placed on
the "rubber sheet" of space-time, making a very deep
dip in the sheet. The dip would be so deep that
nothing could escape from it. In the same way, the
gravity inside a black hole is so strong that nothing—
not even light—can escape from it.

GLOSSARY

Acceleration The rate at which velocity changes with time.

Amplitude The distance from the top of a wave crest to the middle of the wave.

Atom The smallest part of an element that has all the properties of that element.

Center of gravity The point in a object around which its weight is evenly balanced.

Decelerate A slowing, or decrease, in speed.

Density The mass of a substance compared to its volume, or mass per unit volume.

Electron A tiny particle with a negative electric charge that circles the nucleus of an atom.

Energy The ability to do work.

Equilibrium A situation in which opposing forces are balanced and, therefore, no change in movement takes place.

Force A push or pull that starts, stops, or changes the motion of an object.

Frequency The number of times a motion is repeated in one second.

Friction The force that resists movement, and produces heat, when two surfaces are rubbed together.

Fulcrum The point around which a lever turns or pivots.

Gravity The force that draws any two bodies together.

Inertia The tendency for an object to resist being moved or, if moving, to resist a change in its speed or direction.

Magnetic field The space around a magnet where the magnetic effects can be felt.

Magnetic pole The place on a magnet where the magnetic effect is strongest.

Mass The amount of matter in an object.

Molecule The smallest unit into which a substance can be divided and still keep the characteristics of the substance.

Moment The turning effect of a force.

Momentum A property of a moving body that is equal to the mass of the object multiplied by its velocity.

Newton The unit used to measure the size of a force; the force needed to accelerate a mass of 1 kilogram (2.2 ft) by 1 meter (3.5 ft) per second per second.

Nucleus The cluster of particles at the center of an atom.

Pendulum A body that hangs from a fixed point and is free to swing.

Period The time taken for one complete cycle of a repeated sequence of events.

Power The rate of doing work, or the rate of transfer of energy.

Resultant force The single force that has the same effect as several forces acting separately in an object.

Speed The rate at which something moves.

Subatomic particle One of the smaller particles—electrons, protons, and neutrons—that make up an atom.

Velocity Speed in a certain direction.

Vibration A regular back and forth movement.

Weight The force exerted on an object by gravity.

Work The amount of energy used when a force is used to move an object.

FURTHER INFORMATION

BOOKS TO READ

Crump, Donald J., ed. *Fun with Physics* (Books for World Explorers Series 7: No. 4). National Geographic Society, 1986.

DePinna, Simon. *Forces and Motion* (Science Projects series.) Raintree Steck-Vaughn, 1998.

Grimshaw, Caroline. *Energy* (Invisible Journeys series). World Book, 1998.

Riley, Peter D. *Forces of Movement* (Straightforward Science series). Franklin Watts, 1998.

Sauvain, Philip. Motion (Way It Works series). Simon & Schuster Children's, 1992.

WEB SITES

http://www.fnal.gov/
Home page for the U.S. Department of Energy's Fermilab, a global research and educational center exploring the fundamental nature of matter and energy.

http://sln.fi.edu
Franklin Institute Science Museum

http://www.phylink.com/fun.cfm
Physics and Science Fun, by PhysLink

http://ericir.syr.edu/Projects/Newton
Newton's Apple, (PBS family science program) ideas for science projects.

Forces acting on a moving object

Burning rocket fuel creates a force that pushes the rocket upward.

Friction caused by moving through the air slows down the rocket.

The force of gravity pulls the rocket toward the Earth.

FORCES AND MOTION – Quantities and units

Basic quantities

Quantity	Symbol	Basic SI unit	Abbreviation
Mass	m	kilogram	kg
Length	l	meter	m
Time	t	second	s
Current	I	ampere	A

Derived quantities (these are based on those above)

Quantity	Symbol	Equation or definition	Unit name and abbreviation	Derived SI unit
Velocity	v	velocity = distance ÷ time	–	$m\ s^{-1}$
Acceleration	a	acceleration = velocity ÷ time	–	$m\ s^{-2}$
Force	F	force = mass x acceleration	Newton (N)	$kg\ m\ s^{-2}$
Work	W	work = force x distance	Joule (J)	N m
Energy	E	Capacity to do work	–	Joule
Power	P	power = work done ÷ time	Watt (W)	$J\ s^{-1}$
Area	A	(Depends on shape)	–	m^2
Volume	V	(Depends on shape)	–	m^3
Density	ρ	density = mass ÷ volume	–	$kg\ m^{-3}$
Pressure	P	pressure = force ÷ area	Pascal (Pa)	$N\ m^{-2}$
Period	T	Time taken for one cycle	–	s
Frequency	f	Number of cycles per second	Hertz (Hz)	s^{-1}
Momentum	–	momentum = mass x velocity	–	$kg\ m\ s^{-1}$
Electric charge	Q	charge = current x time	Coulomb (C)	A s